Notes on Endings

Notes on Endings

Clare Banks

Terrapin Books

© 2025 by Clare Banks
Printed in the United States of America.
All rights reserved.
No part of this book may be reproduced in any manner,
except for brief quotations embodied in critical articles
or reviews.

Terrapin Books
4 Midvale Avenue
West Caldwell, NJ 07006

www.terrapinbooks.com

ISBN: 978-1-947896-83-3
Library of Congress Control Number: 2025937512

First Edition

Cover art by Vincent Van Gogh
Landscape with Wheelbarrow
watercolor on cream paper
Courtesy of the Cleveland Museum of Art

Cover design by Diane Lockward

for my mother and my sisters

Contents

Bower of Bliss   3

I
Franck Avenue, Louisville   7
Blue Jay   8
Late March Aubade   9
Burned House   11
Having Lost Your Daughter   12
Good Things Are Coming   13
Our Island Camp   15

II
Against Memory   19
Notes on Beech Hill Pond   20
On Location   22
Four to Midnight   24
Georgia Avenue   26
Lake Swim   27
Canoeing   29
A Cliff Over Foster Falls   30

III
A Hike   35
Winter Wilderness   36
It Does No Good   37
Lying to My Father   38
Lying About Your Father   39
Secret Smoker   40
Reservoir   41

IV
A Trick, a Lure, a Gift	45
We Consider Moving to a Campground	48
Glass Tree House	50
Morning on the Eastern Shore	51
Playing in the Pastoral Dream	52
About Loss	54
The Fates	55
My Mother on Her Knees	56

V
Notes on Endings	59

VI
Summer in the Fern Garden	73
At Night	74
Thanksgiving Day	75
The Savage Gulf	76
We Remember for You	78
Elegy for Exile	80

Acknowledgments	83
About the Author	85

It is a place as real as the imagination is real, both a moment and memory.

—Stanley Plumly

Bower of Bliss

Last night at the play, as the father/actor stood crying,
counting the reasons he could not go on

and the friend/actress counted back
reasons to forgive death's injustice,

I found myself thinking about who I must forgive:
my sister for dying? How can I begin.

Maybe forgiveness isn't the right word.
Disease, I know, with its splitting cells,

in which blind tumors reel and slake their hunger,
is out of my hands, doesn't care what I want.

What if I forgave the summer instead?
The nasturtium stems tangled in their pots,

the spikes of cardinal flower hanging
over the walk where mulberries like manna rot, vinegar-sweet.

In the branches above, all manner of birds rest,
feast, sluice through the small, curling leaves, fences,

the neighborhood painted in their purple shit,
year after year. Toward the end, my sister sat on her porch

watching the trees flutter, weighted with the thrum of all those songs,
the morning sun low, the air warming by the minute,

floating in its calm sea, insisting on the slowness
of oblivion, time out of time that inches:

sunlight on leaf, water in air, bee stumbling among
blossom, a world cast in gold, brass, green.

Don't move, I think, barely breathe. In this moment
there is nothing broken, nothing shattered,

nothing worth your counting. Why can't we lie?
Refuse the world that drifts, dims and pales,

the night that turns cold, covers us in frost,
that hushes us to sleep.

I

Franck Avenue, Louisville

Rain, I guess, though it could be cold enough
for snow. They're looking up, away from the camera,

smiling. My mother, hair piled on her head,
my father in thick frames. They each hold one

of my sisters, whose hair is cygnet down,
whose small brows furrow, eyes squinting into

the gray light. On this day of nothing much,
I'll leave them, in the face of what I think

I see hovering at the picture's edge.
They stand in the yard of their first house,

an old oak swaying above, where their losses
haven't begun to collect. In this light,

they might toss a girl into the air,
and expect her, like the spring, to return.

Blue Jay

His poem printed with a blue jay hangs
on your son's wall. That you measured the distance
between door and window, pounded a nail
into the plaster, and leveled the angle
of the frame, that you allow it to remain
at all, quietly, a bird on a branch,
blue crest against cream paint, feathers in pale leaves,
is a kind of forgiveness. You might read
it at night when your boy is sleeping, his light
wings folded under his sheet, you might return
to the indecipherable word. Flutter?
No: feather or fault. Your father's tilted
capitals blurred, crowded, his hand beginning
to rush, his poem at the end in flight.

Late March Aubade

Driving home from the airport
in blue sky and sun, marsh grasses
bending along the highway

where the road sinks into the harbor
tunnel, fathoms of bay water
above, the tiled walls tell us,

stay in lane. Cars with waking
drivers line up beneath
container ships on the surface,

sea birds floating in the current.
I've left my mother to fly home,
the blood from the bruise

around her eye where she'd fallen
dissipating, waves of yellow
and red from her brow to her cheekbone.

What nothing did we talk about
on this biting Sunday—plans
for her garden, the essays

I have to grade? There must be something
more to the spring than this.
The world comes into color,

the gray of winter cannot
be fixed. See, there where I surface:
a swath of flowering cherries

and pears along the pock-marked
road, daffodils in the median,
yellow trumpets beating back the wind.

Burned House

Remember the speed of evening
water and salt in the pot

steam on the window
darkness and the house afloat in it

your mother's face swimming in the glass
where she read in the lamplight

or sat on her bed looking out
sleep promises an easing

to hold us still
breath upon breath

where the sounds of night
collect like water in a cave

the ship of our memory
ruins scattered in the grass

Having Lost Your Daughter

You stepped past the damp bricks growing moss,
your hanging flowers dropping petals
and last night's rain. The day's heat rose through
the raspberry canes that line your lawn;
it bore down from the sun rising over
the field to walk with you into the park's locusts
and sweet gums.
              Then, a doe, the early light refracting
in gold leaf around her, as if she were some
holy animal, brought here from a medieval
triptych. Her fawn, its stalk legs folded,
you said, lay some feet behind her, each step
she took stretched the distance.
                            He was small,
sleeping in the uncut grass, he didn't know
he was alone. But she was sick, you thought.
Dying, you guessed. And tired, she must've been
so tired. What was there to do but leave him?

Good Things Are Coming

On this steaming morning after a day
of storms, we've stopped to watch
chainsaws divide a massive branch
of willow oak that's fallen

across the street and yet still lives
in a sort of mid-state—
separated from its body,
its flat green leaves point

out the direction of the wind.
It's here that my son tells
me the story of Asclepius,
healer of the sick, who

brings the dead back to life. He's reading
his way through the stars
this summer and it's got him thinking
about swift punishments,

irrevocable fates—
Asclepius, like the mortal tree,
extinguished by lightning
bolt. He asks if the tree

will live as we turn onto a street
of condemned rowhouses where
here and there a paulownia
grows from rifts in the sidewalk,

a broken upper-story window.
On a cement-covered
wall, block letters in teal paint
rise like a cymbal

crash from a cloudy wash of pink—
good things are coming,
it says, like the voice of the believer
willing a body from the brink.

In the hospital room, I couldn't close
the mouth of my dead.
Instead, I kissed her forehead,
though I should've begged, *Wait, please wait.*

Our Island Camp

Our oars dip and drag against the current.
At the lake's edge, I see ferns,
cardinal flower, and red maples reaching.

We peer into the woods. Darkness,
white-tailed deer moving silently as ghosts
through the underbrush close enough to see us,

close enough to run. A floating metal
shadow, we're trolling clouds of sunfish,
snapping turtles, cottonmouths.

Our children skate their fingers along
the surface, whispering in their hoarse voices
about islands, camps, how to gut fish

and build fires. They say they'll thatch
their roof from thin branches and mud,
cook fish in hot ashes, and hide

their canoe in a thicket of rhododendron.
But I won't leave them here in the dark,
as they wish, by the small beach and woods

beginning. The lake's floor sinks where they walk
and turns out schools of minnows. When they step
to the pier, each time they jump, it's a surprise.

They surface gasping at an underworld
of filtering light, quickly lost, unknowable,
where they're somehow altered, somehow less my own.

II

Against Memory

The sun is out. I'm sitting
on the back step not thinking.
There are new finches

in the hydrangea, but
today, they aren't metaphors.
I promised you I wouldn't see

what's not there.
My sister isn't a doe, peering
around the fence,

my father is no ghost traipsing
up the path. Today, the dead
are dead and I'm sitting in the sun.

Look at me refusing them.

Notes on Beech Hill Pond

Blur of pines and boulders lining
the shore, throwing voices
from cabins across the water.
Bluegill by the dock, their mouths
like the centuries, the shape of hunger.

Mother jay on the porch railing
stalking moths caught
between window and screen.
Her desire worth flying
headlong into glass.

Or, paddling along thin spines
of birches, leaves hanging
like hearts strung. When I fall in,
the cold water is a jolt to my chest.
I think—breathe, swim, breathe.

Where lupine grows along
the wayside with ferns, wild roses,
thousands of sapling hemlocks,
my daughter walks with me, watching
for life scattering in the brush.

A loon across the lake calls
from dark water. Then several voices echo
here, here, and she skims the surface
toward them, the sound a lament.
No, relief; she thought she'd lost them.

On Location

On a small bridge over a fake canal,
I looked upon a model island covered

in long, Floridian grasses. A great blue heron
with its bead of an eye staring out

over the blades stood, gray head feathers
a little oily, wild. Cheap hotel, cheap lagoon,

down-on-its-luck bird, and me alone
with my conference badge blowing around my neck

on its royal blue lanyard. I wished us
on the beach, far from the Pizza Hut to-go shack

behind us in its nest of palms. Or rather,
I wished me away. How could I speak for a bird

awaiting tourist trash? Or maybe I looked
at the bird and saw myself: stranded,

in need of a bath, wondering what possessed her
to land in St. Petersburg where the air

is a weighted blanket. Maybe some places
are just better than others. Unmasked,

they don't ask you to entertain illusions.
For example, I was paddling on the Chesapeake,

a late afternoon spotting turtles sunning
themselves near the shore, and, would you believe it,

a heron, who'd stood at the edge of the water,
spooked and took off, her feathers like slate blue fabric,

the sound of her flapping wings a heavy whoosh
carried back to my canoe. I watched her

long body slipping low along the current.
Her eyes searching the water, the arum

or cordgrass, calculating the depths
of fish beneath the water's salt and murk.

What fish? Which muddy beach? I can't say I remember.
In that way, I suppose it's an illusion, too,

steering to shore, my flip-flops squelching clouds
from the marsh bottom as we drag the boats in.

He catalogs turtles seen, I scratch mosquito bites,
and the evening spins out as we believe them to.

Four to Midnight

The summer I lived with my sister,
Amanda, she worked nights at her school's
computer lab. During the hours
I waited for her, I watched *Star Trek*

reruns, wondering at the landscapes
of distant planets made from fabric
and paint and the odd stretchy
uniforms I was sad we'd all wear

in the future. Outside, there were lightning
bugs, the thrum of 18-wheelers
on the bypass, and stars as thick
as swarms. Sometimes, when I was brave,

I'd stand with the dog, testing the atmosphere
of the driveway and maybe take
enough steps to reach the road
before turning back. I'd imagine

walking past the pine woods, our neighbor's
beached RV, and the stone fraternity
houses, where summer students sat
on porches with bourbon and beer.

The computer lab was a half-mile
from our house and the distance
seemed to stretch, like each breath
pushed it away from us.

I concentrated on the dog's collar
clanking against his tags, the heat
radiating off the asphalt
into the soles of our feet. I knew

there would be no congratulations,
but was sure Amanda would let us wait
with her and her 20 screens for midnight,
when the clocks tipped us closer to daylight

and she'd walk with us through the darkness
toward home. I would watch the hood
of stars and imagine each step
moving us to the end of summer

when my mother would return,
when oak and hickory leaves would dry
on the ground and pale yarrow would rise
at the roadside to the height of my hands.

Georgia Avenue

The gravel driveway was lined
with crackling August grasses,
crickets, katydids singing

through the heat. The tire swing hung
in an oak near the machine yard
at the street's dead end

and the pines toward the bypass
where semis would brake, downshifting
their way to the valley,

the road descending through blown-out rock.
Green light played on the porch floor,
sun coming through the wavy

fiberglass roof where we rested,
our bodies tinted
the algal shade of summer leaves.

There was nowhere to be. No or else
to consider. We slugged Cokes
from cans, our sugared mouths stung.

Lake Swim

We walk through sand pocked with cigarettes
to the beach where thin waves lap

and grasshoppers in the reeds shock the air
with their constant static. My sisters lie

on their towels gleaming in baby oil, smoking,
drinking Cokes, a *Damn the Torpedoes*

cassette blaring from their boombox.
The lake floor feels slick, algae and mud squeeze

between my toes drawing clouds. I swim
along the humming surface with the dog

to the cool waters of the lake's center
where the crack of dragonflies land and lurch away.

The smell of dry earth, dry grasses blowing in
from the fields beyond. My sisters call out,

Don't go too far. I see my legs treading
water past the bulrushes and minnows.

Watch out for the dead horse. A body I picture
lying below me, her brown mane spread

against the lake bottom, each strand playing
in the murky green light of the current.

Canoeing

At the low riverbank, our canoes
hung at the surface, drifting
in the current. We ate sandwiches,
soft cheese on dark bread,
drinking water from dry storage.
The sun, the first in days, warmed
us under orange life vests,
reminding us what summer
was really like. The cool rain
of the week before
distant, nearly forgotten,
as if I hadn't lived through
those days, but arrived here
on this river out of nowhere,
as if this moment by the marsh
grasses and orchards, too, wouldn't
be parceled and fixed in my memory
with other rivers, other canoes,
lunches in early summer,
and an older sister steering
with me in the bow. With each stroke
of my paddle, on any given river,
they hush in my ear, *Silently,*
silently, don't let the cottonmouths hear us.

A Cliff Over Foster Falls

He whines and pants, too scared
to take a step, knowing what he's done,
how he's misjudged the width

of the ledge, its brittle stone,
and the weight of his body.
He's been off his leash, cantering,

searching the brush, nose in the leaves,
then back to us like a game,
like he's herding us, his quarry

moving across the plateau.
It's late fall and the azaleas
and laurel have long since bloomed,

where they wait along the trails,
green-leaved and anonymous.
Hemlocks line the gorge, growing

out from the edge like divers
ready to jump into the pool
sixty feet below. The trail

is littered with their short
needles and miniature cones.
If you were looking down

from the top of a tree,
you'd see him running, you'd notice
his smile, his jaw gaping,

then his confusion at the edge,
looking into deep water,
a hole in the mountain,

like a cave pried open,
its lid thrown. He stands struggling
to leap back, you can see it

in his hind legs, how they think
to jump higher, then lose faith
and stall out. I'm sure he'll fall.

As my sister picks her way
lower along the cliff,
hanging onto steady trees,

she reaches for his collar,
to bring him back to us,
and in this moment, I picture

them sliding, the scrape of loose earth
and skree in our ears, their drop
into the falls, where we search

the cave's water for them,
but we're blind in blind water,
we've lost them to the leaves.

III

A Hike

We ditch our bikes off the path
to roam in the woods and find her—
a drawing of a naked woman—

carved into the gray-green lichen
boiling over exposed rock.
Her legs are monstrous and spread

open, her dumb mouth riveted
in a smile, her hair like Betty
or Veronica, toes set against

the stone in a cartoonish
wriggling. With our tennis shoes,
we kick at the curved lines

of her breasts, her nipples, her eyes
that taunt our flat chests.
Then, thinking of the Samaritan,

who comes across the man beaten
and stripped in the road. I consider
covering her with leaves,

that we could offer her a kindness,
bury her image in earth.
But I don't. I pick up my bike and run.

Winter Wilderness

Snow in the late afternoon. It's mid-December
and evening is beginning to dim its gray
light over the mountain. We've trudged

into the wilderness looking for a stand of cedars,
for one to cut and drag through the woods
to our house, back where the road meets the trees.

My mittens are stiff and cold on my hands
with the frozen remnants of snowballs
I've hurled at my sisters who are no longer

speaking to me. I run among the trees
while they dig their saw into the fibers
of cedar bark. Through the snow and mounds

of fallen leaves, I imagine crossing
a threshold, to a world where the voices
of my family are dampened and far-off,

the light around them dusk reflecting
off the snow. I wonder who am I now
that I am beyond their reach? Who will I become?

Mercenary or queen? A mother like mine?
She reads to us at night in the cold,
our hands warmed by burning kerosene.

It Does No Good

I can see him sitting with my mother
        on the porch, the sunlight coming

through the green fiberglass roof,
        which made their faces alien

though I could read them well enough—
        quietly fuming, harsh words, hushed tones.

I watched through a window
        standing on a chair, behind me a sister

stretching to see—*what are they saying?*
        What are they saying?

I'll think of this years later when I wake
        from a dream through which he's found me—

a mute ghost whose mouth can move,
        whose words will not take note.

I watch as his hands turn up to show
        what he can give and that's what strikes me,

how he cradles the emptiness,
        how he's mistaken it for hope.

Lying to My Father

I'm home alone when my father calls.
It's dark out so I can't see beyond

my reflection in the kitchen window,
the fluorescent light above me ticking.

I can hear his voice, sober, quietly
holding mine to his ear. I'm scared he will

make the five-hour trek, come barreling up
the mountain in his truck, that he will appear

in our driveway, Linda Ronstadt blaring.
That he will make us go back to Louisville

and his silent apartment where his neighbor's cat
whines on the fire escape. *Where's your mother?*

he asks instead and I fall into place on the linoleum,
a hot rush of panic gathering in my chest, arms.

Working, I lie. I must hide her from him.
He hangs in a moment between breakdowns,

like a black hole forming, a light
that whitens, collapses, turns utterly dark.

Lying About Your Father

You don't know why you say it—*he's dead*—
why you lie and murder him in the abstract.
You're angry, you're young, some kid asked
where he is, why he doesn't live with you,
and *Screw this*, you think, picturing him
at Our Lady of Peace, drying out, *he's dead*.
Fall on the main road, the one with a stoplight,
you stand across the street from the market,
in a group of kids on their way home,
a glass bottle of Coke in your hand.
Slick bubbles swell in your stomach,
the lie, like foul air, rising. There are leaves
on the pebbled sidewalk and you, stuck
in the frame, with your mouth open—your small,
dark heart thrumming in your throat.

Secret Smoker

My mother kept her Benson & Hedges
in a cabinet between the kitchen
and TV room—an alcove too small

for adults to fit. Alone, I'd sidle in and pull
the drawer—gold and silver boxes arranged
in rows. Making sure the house

was silent, I'd slide a long cigarette
from an open pack. Her lighter a trick
with my thumb, its flame a step past taboo.

With the filter at my lips, I'd suck the smoke
into my mouth and practice sending
it into my lungs and out through my nose.

My mouth a sour tart, I'd play at flicking
ashes into the tray, spinning the coals
at the end to a smoldering point.

I was precise, terrifyingly bold.
Expecting the weight of my mother's tires
on the gravel drive, I'd light another.

Reservoir

I'm nineteen, waiting in my car
in the pitch dark, eyes closed,
listening for his cut ignition,
shoes on gravel, and the weight
of him on the seat next to me.
As if we'd met here before,
as if I'd learned this
as a sequence. I remember
walking here with my sister.
Our wet hair in clumps, towels wrapping
our shoulders after swimming.
We stopped to pick roadside
raspberries from bees and thorns,
our hands stained pink.
And once, with Girl Scouts, deer tracks
stretching the beach, the damp sand
turned up by hooves all the way
to the woods. I could see
their brown flanks against
the understory, their white tails.
I want to leave one man
for another in this place
where listening for his nearness,
I imagine the huff of his breath
in my ear. By dawn, I've slept,
a mist hanging above the water,
sunlight beginning. He hasn't come.
I drive away through trees and trees.

IV

A Trick, a Lure, a Gift

What looks like a wolf walks through the Piazza
Venezia, her long legs bent at knobby joints,

resigned on her leash, hang-dog eyes waiting
for her moment, as in the Forum's pocked walls,

green parrots knock each other out of the shaded,
cramped niches, the trees above my bench rattle

with their bickering exile. We each bear our loneliness
like heat among the ruins. I search for the Temple

of Castor and Pollux, brothers who understand
the lot of a sibling without its mate, like breathing

at the bottom of the world. I take what I can get.
When the trinket sellers approach, I wonder

who they are now so far from where they began.
Each moment an exercise in imagination —

their homelands, the way their language perks their ears,
like birds calling across an expanse of trees.

Can I hear your voice or have I made it up?
I cannot remember truly, each thought,

each looking back distorts, puts the truth
that much farther out of reach. At Santa Maria

in Cosmedin by the Tiber, I descend
to the crypt—cool, damp, sulfurous air that knocks

me back. There is a passage behind Hercules' altar
through the ancient tufa from which the dead

could send false dreams. Are they a trick, a lure, or a gift?
When I step out of the church's dim light

into the smack of day and stand amidst the fact
of plane trees, I know their leaves are wide like sheaves of paper,

as fragile as skin. At a market stall, I buy peaches,
each knot of fruit like fresh flowers,

which, if you were here, you'd toss by threes
into the air, juggle as smaller suns against a sky so blue

to look at it is pain. In the street lined with motorbikes,
the litter of broken leaves, and evening settling,

I picture this life as mine—my cafe, my apartment,
my station—where I walk into the street,

know the scent from the doorways, the words bubbling
in spray paint along the walls. Where I walk

in and out of the air and fit. Warm tiles under my feet,
hanging sheets to dry between afternoon storms,

inside my body ticking with breath
in the nothingness of each moment.

But, sister, I cannot truck such dreams.
You are here, you are here, you are nowhere.

We Consider Moving to a Campground

A brackish river banked by orange trees
flowering, the scent trailing past
as we broke camp, tent poles folded
and bagged, sleeping bags jigsawed

into the trunk. We'd showered off
the cocktail of Deet and Hawaiian Tropic
in the bathhouse and dressed for the drive
to Tennessee, 11 hours, backwards

from summer to spring. Against
the Delta 88's soft brocade seats,
I sweat in comfort, my face,
like a dog's, in the open window,

sand in drifts at my feet. First, boulevards
of Waffle Houses, storage centers,
strip clubs, then the turn for a last look
at the gulf, a coast road buffeted

by privet, banyan, and red cedar.
We paused there where my sisters
pipedreamed a Jet Ski rental
and a wooden pier bayside

where we fished our dinner out
of the salt water and muck—speckled
trout, sea bream—we could leave
the present, escape to a campground,

nights reading westerns around
a fire, days shelling the beach,
as if the sun was the thing that lifted us,
that held our future in such relief.

Glass Tree House

On the top floor of the house, high in the trees,
        rain gathers on the warped and rusty screens.

The river runs by, some small, silent artery
        from the Chester and the Chesapeake before that.

My sisters dive off the dock in the rain to swim
        with the blue crabs they're trying to catch

in old metal traps. I want to go out there, jump
        after them, into the murk with the snakes,

the fish, their sloughed-off scales, and the muddy river
        bottom. They pull themselves onto an abandoned

pier, on the far side of the water, its wood black
        and rotting, and lie down like turtles sunning

themselves, though there's nothing but clouds and gray light.
        I want to hear what they're saying,

to know the words I don't recognize. Their chatter
        comes like static dampened and thrown

by the wind through the rain, I catch
        a flicker, a laugh, then like that, I lose them.

Morning on the Eastern Shore

In the shallows, slender pondweed bends, catches white, pliant jellyfish,
        their filmy bodies like small, scattered lungs.

Across the inlet, tall pines line the shore and herons scan the surface
        for the shadows of fish and crab where the sun

has burned off the fog from dawn. When you woke up, you watched
        light bring the things of the world into focus—

fish hook, chestnut, beer can—the winter waiting in the leaves, the outline
        of the oaks breaking from the bluing sky.

In the emptiness of the house and yard, you notice something like time
        hanging, though there's nothing you can do to slow

this life, to dull this sense of an ending. You're on a pier, the water
        laps beneath you, the breeze playing in a spider's web

near your knee. You can see that the wake disturbs the muddy shallows,
        the morning touches everything, then turns away.

Playing in the Pastoral Dream

My neighbor spent the summer destroying
his yard. Lopping the tops of his trees,
and razing the ground until it was no more
than dirt, the roots of vines ascending

like wire. I was on the sidewalk
watching my kids ride bikes when his wife
came onto their porch in a bathrobe.
Her head behind the screen was pale and bald

from what could only be chemo.
My body seized at the sight of her,
and I thought of my sister last winter
in her wig. It's no use, I wanted

to tell him. There's no construction,
no revision that will stop this.
In the street it was dusk: I knew about death
and I didn't. It hardly mattered.

The red brush of a cardinal darted
across my yard in the evening's odd coolness,
moving to her nest in the hedgerow.
Sycamores lining the street shed bark

like snakes in wide strokes, leaving their trunks
a pale green. Inside my pastoral dream,
the white noise of cicadas rises
around my son playing in the grass.

The street lies awash in golden light
like that of endless spring. And my daughter,
at the end of the block, she's a deer
wandering the trees, she's in and out of sight.

About Loss

This year's not the story you want to tell.
You want it to be someone else's tragedy
and probably it is: you haven't cornered

the market on loss. You think about standing
in the hot attic in your summer rags
and flip-flops in a deep sweat, the scent

of lemons and garlic on your hands from dinner.
If you go downstairs, you'll find your family
sitting outside, the night's fireflies a net

they're caught in. If you stay where you are,
by your mother's sewing machine and neat
piles of fabric, the sloping attic

ceiling, you'll turn to stone. And which is better?
A place on the porch where the wind doesn't
move, your wine glass dripping in your hand,

or your body rooted, like the Medusa
who saw herself: fierce, terrible, frozen.

The Fates

They gather around her stitching,
fine threads through needle eyes.

There's daylight left, though it's fading.
Shadows slipping to this sister's side.

They find she's poisoned through and through,
wants nothing more, or something more?

Go, don't look at me; stay, don't move,
she breathes. The knots mount in their laps

like lives, like loves, each distinct,
a pattern complete. This woman

on the brink—should they take her, cut
her wretched breathing? Listen:

there's no language left in their calls,
just a keening spilling from the mother's mouth.

My Mother on Her Knees

her face and hands in a bed
of iris their leaves sharp
fans her focus a blotting out
of noise of light she pulls
dry tubers their roots
like something left too long
on the sill something
forgotten there is something
she must remember keep hold
of the flowers cut back
the dying green split the tangled
bodies seamed at their bulbous curves
it is not late or too late
she is not in the street yelling
that her daughter is dead
she has not run from the house
into the hum of the evening
where the tree frogs trill
she is in the dusk of her garden
camellia rose mint in her nails
like shovels she is on her knees
on the flagstones the heady
green in the light like gold

V

Notes on Endings

August

I remember her floating back and forth
on the tire, kicking off from the tree trunk,
her hands red from the rope's sharp,

fraying threads. The dog panting
in the shade eyed every thunk
from her feet and short crack as shards

of bark fell away. The sun weighed
on the neighbor's corn and still we stayed,
the shrill cicadas rose to a fever, then sank.

September

Like Ariadne, we unspooled our thread,
wrapped tree trunks to mark our zig-zagged
path from the house through the woods.

Somewhere there'd be a crack in a boulder,
a drop approaching in the dusk.
Looking for wood smoke above the fading

summer trees, we searched what was left
of the light, expecting the minotaur
waiting at the cave's mouth.

October

A crush of children on the sidewalks
running to houses in the near dark.
Doorbells, candy in pillowcases,

costumes unraveling, detritus left
like storm trash blown across the grass.
A headdress, a mask, a necklace of jewels.

November

Last trip to New York—her hair hanging on
through a new chemo how she laughed
when I sprayed her part with dry shampoo

like cornstarch thickening, amateurs, we tried
to style the clumps—she's strong, I thought
knowing the opposite was true.

December

I searched for smooth pebbles on the winter beach
scraping them free of wet sand with my hands, then,
she said, pull your arm back, rock between

thumb and forefinger—her arm on my arm,
hand around my hand, the flat side facing the ground—
I tossed it across the surface. She counted

the skips, hits that radiated circles,
all the way to the lake's center. I stood
watching her watch the stones carve the cold breeze.

January

Ice covered every knob and crevice. Tree
branches sagged under the weight and dragged against
the ground's frozen sheet. Their clanging a muffled

and tuneless carillon or changes rung
by a frigid wind. The power cut out,
of course, and we spent days in the cold house—

one room warmed with burning kerosene.
We breathed fresh air on the porch, galling
and damp, it pierced like needles.

February

Crocus, snowdrops, sprays of daffodils
in otherwise empty beds: cues to clear
the dry trash from fall, stalks, tall dormant spikes.

She planned the garden, a map of squares, raised
blocks: herbs and tomatoes here, nasturtium
and cut flowers there. By August, they'd grow

higher than our heads, flowers sending seeds
like filament into the afternoon,
no one could bear to bring them down.

March

Last things, last words worth saying, how I'd load
them into the bubble on my phone,
delete them, start again. If only our

speech was like that, mutable, easily
erased. Like when I asked her
for the truth: would she die? And she sat

on the edge of the couch and said, *yes,
this year*, and I wanted them back, the words,
as if by scouring them, I'd keep her close.

April

I walked too close, held her arm. She shook
me off, unwilling to be given up.
Trillium, cinquefoil, and jack-in-the-pulpit

bloomed on the muddy bank of the creek.
She was there and not there, as if she
were fading; as if she were choosing to fade.

May

On the patio with drinks, dinner, the sun
filtering through her pink linen dress.
Silk scarf wrapping tropical birds around

her head, her hair like down, like thread-bare clouds
underneath. She stood in the sunlight,
smiling, her body still a mystery.

June

The cabin's trees slowed their waving, rain
tapered, and the air settled into silence.
The sun broke the clouds apart

and, here and there, a wood thrush began to call.
Cicadas answered in the damp grass,
the mountain breathing, awake.

July

Maraschino cherries in our mother's fridge.
I remember the taste of them from a party years ago.
I twisted the sticky lid from the jar,

snuck them one by one through that summer,
a sweet that lingered in my teeth. I slide them
from the cool door, hold them, put them back.

She's saving them for her yellow cake
with egg-white icing, cherries and paper flags
like the wings of mourning cloaks across the top.

VI

Summer in the Fern Garden

It's the end of summer in the fern garden
and every morning starts the same—
the rain letting up or pouring again.

It's difficult to tell which will happen
first—daylight seeping through the canopy,
turning the ferns a shade lighter,

or the day's first deer disappearing
at the clearing's edge. Once the sun is out
and the roads are steaming, we listen

to rustling in the trees, a doe picking
her way through the woods. For a second,
I let myself imagine it's Carrie,

just back from a walk: light
on the steps, leaves flagging the drive,
rain that spills from the road to the creek.

At Night

At night they skim the pine board floors,
the only others awake
in the cabin's silence. As they travel
the cupboards and shelves

gathering in their teeth what they
can carry, you find you're
thinking in the cadence of her
voice, that you hear her cleaning

on a morning three years ago,
taking down the porch spider's
webs before the family woke up
and became ensnared

in them. That she's here at all
is the movement of her
syllables across space to your ears
or time somehow collapsing.

And don't you wish you could get out
of bed, walk outside
and find her, that all you had
to do was wake the dead.

Thanksgiving Day

This morning after frost
there is still so much alive.
The leaves darker, traced in white
in the sunlight, curl, keep close
to the ground. The smell, too,
the mud in the yard, a cold
camellia's note drifting.
How can I walk inside
to the other life, to my mother
and sisters cooking
and leave this moment
in the garden, a cold morning
with nothing broken.

The Savage Gulf

We stood looking out to the bare trees
along the river. Shallow water lapping like breath

on the smooth pebbles, a fish here and there
darting, flicking muscled tails to hide

among the rocks. The smell of skunk cabbage
catching me over and over, bloodroot twisting

from downed leaves and the thawing earth.
It's here, still in coats, in March, that I remember

a hike with Carrie, who, trail map in hand,
led us lost through the Savage Gulf

as the sun began to set behind the mountains
dun-colored in November. We walked

along the bluff for hours, up and down hollows
and crevices following one color of blazes,

then another, pulling the six-year-old
and the dog away from every edge.

As our phones faltered and daylight faded,
she stopped to consult the map again

and turned us toward a three-mile trek that ended
at the car in twilight where we laughed it off

drinking water, pounding snacks: our brush with death.
We'd heard stories about lost hikers,

we knew their chances, imagined the search parties
sent for us: five adults, a boy, a dog.

Someone had usually fallen and broken
an ankle, but we'd broken nothing, we said,

how lucky, how lucky we are. But who wasn't thinking,
as we laughed in the face of it, that Carrie

was already dying. We knew she was terminal.
Instead, I asked about place names—Beersheba,

Gruetli-Laager, Stone Door.
I wanted to remember them for a poem.

To place us there, to keep us where trees crowd
boulders covered in moss and lichen,

all of us saved to a moment somewhere
behind us. As if she would exist

infinitely, as if she could continue.
It was an evening near Thanksgiving,

and if you were looking at a map, not far
from valleys descending into the west.

We Remember for You

We begin on the highway
or a street even
in a car tightly packed

there is darkness like waking up
or the darkness of a dream

here we move
like birds of prey
or apparitions hunting
though hunting isn't right—
what we do isn't violent—
we search maybe we look for

in the leaves piled against
the trunks of trees
among the beeches hanging on

it is January dark
January with a gray sky above the trail
and though we look
for something light for a lightness
we can't see much
our eyes aren't true

what we want
is to grab with our hands
to bring back something gold
once golden—

here then is what we tell you

we breathe at the cave's mouth
half in darkness half in sunlight
our feet among the pebbles
of the creek bottom

what story there is plays here
clear fish in clear water

Elegy for Exile

Days spent within words, nights listening
to a colony of tree frogs who live

near a forgotten pool, who call
into the canopy, into the streets laid quiet

by darkness, to the foxes nudging
hedges, slinking a path between cars,

it's a song for insomnia, its peculiar exile,
for July and the years spread out between summers,

between life and death, the taste of magnolia
on their tongues, all their small hearts

hanging onto branches, thumping the cadence
of a short life and its collapsed years

in which all manner of miracles must occur.
Is it enough that the trilling feels like a tether,

a line that opens the past, is it enough
to remember her as sound, a lament

called out from the trees? Here, she says,
I'm here. I've never left this vale of leaves.

Acknowledgments

Many thanks to the editors of the magazines in which these poems first appeared, some in earlier versions.

Blue Mesa Review: "Blue Jay"

Boulevard: "A Hike"

The Greensboro Review: "Our Island Camp"

Iron Horse Literary Review: "Having Lost Your Daughter" and "My Mother on Her Knees"

JMWW: "Playing in the Pastoral Dream"

Mississippi Review: "Lying About Your Father"

Poet Lore: "About Loss"

Poetry South: "A Cliff Over Foster Falls" and "Lake Swim"

Radar Poetry: "Bower of Bliss," "Elegy for Exile," "Four to Midnight," and "On Location"

"Playing in the Pastoral Dream" was the "Pick of the Week" feature on the *The Best American Poetry* blog, April 6, 2025.

Thanks to early readers Chris Stewart, Rachel Hicks, and Traci O'Dea who helped shape many of these poems. To Don Berger, Lindsay Bernal, Michael Collier, Mary Jo Salter, Terence Winch, and David Yezzi, I'm grateful for your encouragement and support. Special thanks and love to my mother, Diane; my sisters, Gaia, Amanda, Hosanna, and Carrie, who we lost; and my children, Maeve and August. Much love and appreciation to my husband, Stephen Reichert, with whom everything is possible.

About the Author

Clare Banks is associate editor for *Smartish Pace*. A recipient of two Maryland State Arts Council Individual Artist Awards, her poems have been featured in the *The Best American Poetry* blog, and in such journals as *B O D Y*, *The Louisville Review*, *Mississippi Review*, and *Poet Lore*. She was nominated for the Best New Poets 2023 anthology by *Mississippi Review*, was a 2023 finalist in *Radar Poetry*'s Coniston Prize and a 2024 finalist in *Iron Horse Literary Review*'s National Poetry Month Prize. She has an MFA in poetry from the University of Maryland and lives in Baltimore City where she co-hosts The HOT L Poets Series. *Notes on Endings* is her début full-length collection.

www.ingramcontent.com/pod-product-compliance
Lightning Source LLC
Chambersburg PA
CBHW020442090526
44586CB00045B/768